I0212517

Connections To The Hearts Intentions

Phoenix Walker

Published by New Generation Publishing in 2013

Copyright © Phoenix Walker 2013

First Edition

The author asserts the moral right under the Copyright,
Designs and Patents Act 1988 to be identified as the
author of this work.

All Rights reserved. No part of this publication may be
reproduced, stored in a retrieval system or transmitted,
in any form or by any means without the prior consent
of the author, nor be otherwise circulated in any form
of binding or cover other than that which it is published
and without a similar condition being imposed on the
subsequent purchaser.

www.newgeneration-publishing.com

New Generation Publishing

Dedication

I am devoting this book to a very special lady in my life that passed away suddenly. My mum Carolyn Walker lost her battle with a sudden heart attack on 15.01.2013. She was my greatest role model, she was bulletproof in every respect.

I have been writing poetry since 17 years old when I was struggling with coming to terms that I'm gay. I've experienced heartache, lost many people through tragic circumstances. This I feel makes me able to write from a real place, a raw sense of emotion.

I have a friend Nicholas Ross from Plymouth I would like to thank for his belief in me. Daniel Mizzi my cousin for his editing of my book to give it the feel I wanted.

I am going to be donating money from this book to Plymouth mind who have recently helped me throughout my depression. On a positive note anyone who has a dream, has a life ambition, follow your truth. Plymouth pub bread and roses I would like to thank for allowing me to read out my poems live at mic night to showcase my creative writing.

I would also like to thank Claire Cambridge for her role model as my friend and my manager at Starbucks, who pushed me into a higher sense of confidence.

Poems devoted to Claire our LIGHT and one other poem destiny of a mum to be.

I have some many beautiful people in my life and I feel blessed in my friendships and family.

I hope you enjoy reading this book and I hope different aspects relate to your lives and it did to my life.

Thanks to everyone who continues to believe in me

PHOENIX WALKER

CONNECTIONS TO THE HEARTS INTENTIONS

Spark and Fantastic Light

In chance we meet and conversation leads on for days.
I look into you and see a fragile beautiful heart.
I hear your mistakes and regrets, no one is perfect.
You're this beautiful man due to all that resides in your past.
You continue to evolve each day that fades into the background.
I hear your past, it draws me in and holds my attention.
I have a heart that seems to spark alive in your presence.
Sparks and fantastic rays of light surround your aura.
Your energy is unique in how you see life.
Your eyes see beauty and close over to hate.
I felt a spark and fireworks in our talks.
You have so much more I feel I've yet to discover from you.
My light is fantastic and your spark is infectious.
Your sparks fire me up with excitement.
My light will brighten your world to a whole new way of living.
I feel you and me were meant to connect.
I feel your spark in all that we do.
Chemistry we share is undeniable, respect for you came quickly.
I feel I have met you somewhere before.
I feel this spark and light is just a reconnect.
It feels natural and sets my heart alive with your mystery.
I feel you were sent my way, and I was sent into your life too.
My light and beauty I will share with you.
I will let you in to places not many get to see.
Into my version of life, my version of reality.
This connection so random and out of the blue.

In your eyes I see a sense of adventure you need to
unlock.

I feel my passion and drive will unlock your wild side.

I want to live it up to experience all possible joy.

I feel between my light and your sparks.

This new adventure is about to start.

You spark up my heart and I feel my light opens your
eyes to so much more wonder.

I feel lucky to have come into your world of mystery.

Let's have a journey to the centre of each other's
dreams.

Make all a reality, between my lights and your sparks.

Sleeping Next To You

At night in the arms of only you.

I rest my heart near yours, as you drift off in the safety of dreams.

I see how fragile you appear, losing you my biggest fear.

Sleeping next to you I feel each heartbeat.

Sleeping next to you is as close as two people can be.

Sleeping in your arms I feel a sense of pride and contentment.

Sleeping next to you feels safe and a sense of closeness in your arms.

The world is surrounded by a mad pace, always rushing somewhere

Less silence to enjoy the one you love, hold me and let's forget the world

You appear in my dreams as a vision of beauty inside and out.

Loving you is easy, no mixed signals and no doubt.

Sleeping next to you hours pass us by.

Sleeping next to you I lose my sense of all that surrounds me.

Since the day I surrendered my heart to your life.

Sleeping next to only you is all I wish to do.

Diamond Bulletproof Shield

You were my biggest influence, I never really took in
your wisdom.
I would listen and run in the line of the danger you
warned me of.
I didn't see the tough lessons you wanted me to learn.
I just wanted to be individual, refusing to show you I
loved you.
People would fire bullets at my confidence.
People would lead me down roads far away from your
protection.
As your son, I caused you worry and fear.
As my mum you were always near.
No matter what danger, no matter where.
You had a way of finding me and leading me back on
track.
For that I love you more than anything in this world.
I had times in my life when bullets fired daily on my
self esteem.
You would stand in the way and let them fire their fuel
at your diamond shield.
You were bulletproof mum, you would take pain to
insure I felt no fear.
You were bulletproof when it came to loving me.
You were my biggest influence, I learned the hard way.
That you always know what's best for me.
You could read peoples' intentions for me.
For that I learned how to weigh up situations by
watching you.
I will make you proud mum and prove I've learned
from the best.
Losing you was my biggest test.
As now I only have memories of your guidance for me.
I feel you in my life, I will achieve my goal.

You may have been misunderstood, as you didn't allow many in your heart.

You would rather people fear than love you.

The ones that got past your shield, they saw a heart made of pure gold.

I was allowed into places in your heart that many never saw.

You were a true lady through and through.

I was lucky to have a mum to guide and influence me, I was lucky it was you.

Self

I am what I see in the mirror, I am me and no one can define it.

I am not able to fall from heights just through criticism and stones at my heart.

I am complete within and without someone to hold me at night.

A sense of self is awareness of our own direction.

A sense of self, comes with the confidence life makes us gain from suffering and pain.

A sense of being alive comes when you leave all fear behind.

Self is discovering you're unique and individual, not to explain yourself in judgment's eyes.

Self is being alone but feeling total contentment in your own time and space.

I learned not to let life tear away at my life, leaving me on the ground.

I see strength grow in me, I'm always a new self from that of yesterday.

I look at my mistakes, and learn how to better my awareness of me.

I feel the higher the spirit grows in you, the more self and being becomes much deeper.

All that you feel, let it all be and all energies pass through us.

A sense of self comes when we stop asking too much of ourselves.

A sense of being can be taken if we allow powerful forces to steal from us.

A sense of self when confidence sets in, will make us unbreakable.

A sense of self that leaves us still on a road of learning.

Spiritual awakening and self is something that in our life never will end.

The best you can do is to continue to grow from all that life deals you with.

Self is you, and this is your personal path to go down.

Avoid listening to all the noise and listen to your own frequency.

Self and being you, is a frequency no one else can ever tune into completely.

You're unique and your self and being is yours alone, it belongs to no one.

Stay you, and follow your inner compass, it will always lead to the right way to your self and being you.

My Own Destiny Forgotten

I used to look at the world and have fantastic hope for
my achievable dreams to come alight.

I planned out the way to make my talent from silver
into gold.

I somewhere in my life lost sight I had destiny of my
own.

I spent time giving so many people my time and part of
me.

I felt lost in giving so much to others, my heart began
to die.

I spend time talking for hours to the ones who needed
me, neglecting me.

Every desire I ever had, put on hold as I was investing
in everyone but me.

I would give my partner more and more, allowing me
to suffer and my destiny to fade to grey.

My own destiny got forgotten leaving me feeling I had
no life to live but the lives of others.

When you give so much, people take so much more
from you.

People don't stop to ask, can you spare yourself from
your day or do you need time for you.

The more I valued the destiny and direction of the ones
I loved, the more I lost my way.

One moment of clarity, I cried and became so numb I
could not breathe.

What was I doing, where had I been, but living for
everyone but me.

I took a step from outside the box I was in, and looked
at me from afar.

My destiny, my dreams all had been left on the
roadside in a desert to die.

My own version of life and destiny all forgotten, living
for everyone but me.

I wiped away my tears, learned to stop giving all my emotions to everyone.

Leaving no love in my own heart for me, my own destiny and life almost forgotten.

I started to live for me, I started to breathe for me and no one else.

I still give myself to the ones I love, but only if my own self is taken care of first.

Learning to love one's own life, living for me and not living through others any more.

It made me feel a sense of release, a sense that for once in my life I had found my destiny.

Impossible Prince Charming

I am high maintenance, with a pure heart.

I am impatient, I expect too much sometimes.

I expect the best from my lover, from my man

I've thrown away men for being too easy to throw their heart at me.

Making no game, no chase, not sexy, being so easy to win.

I've thrown away men for not loving this world we all share.

Life is beautiful, can't you see.

I've thrown away the boring man, the controller, the masters of deception.

Silly boys you can't fool me by your lies or try and win me then mistreat me.

Impossible prince charming I may be.

Not many men can handle me.

Impossible prince charming, I guard my heart under lock and key.

Impossible prince charming, if you decode my affection you get my loyalty.

I will give you all the love your mind can handle.

I will protect you and show you this world is full of wonder.

I will open you up, challenge your wishes.

I will remain me, and so should you.

Impossible prince charming I may be too many.

If you decode my heart, get in my life to share all of me.

I will be your prince charming.

Many try, many just get my impossible prince side.

For the special one, you will get my softer side.

You will get the prince you seek.

Love is something that should be given harder than just a few heartbeats.

Love should be given by falling into the same space with another.

I know love is something I won't just give away.

They call me the impossible prince charming as my love needs to be earned.

I seek my diamond in rough to pull my walls down.

I seek the man to give me the real deal.

Till that day, I hide my heart inside this impossible prince charming

Parents Listen One Moment

As a young boy you would do your best to guide me.

Hold me and tell me that everything is alright.

Under your rules and protection I never stopped learning.

I always made sure to be true to me, even when you told me I was wrong.

I was a test on your patience, the individual minded son you didn't expect.

Bullies came into my life to make me fall.

My battle from the ground was long and tough.

In my tears one night I almost made a choice to take my own life away.

To suffer no more, and cause my loved ones no more pain.

Some strength in me told me to carry on and live my life.

Brick by brick I rebuild my self esteem.

Brick by brick I rebuild my confidence and sense of me.

I came out as gay to you, mum and dad.

I know you worried over me and what life would hold in store for me.

I have had love affairs that have shaped me.

I have had love affairs almost break me.

No one will ever change me.

Parents do you worry at night?, if I'm doing alright.

Parents do you know the boy that became a man.

Parents do you know my life plan.

Parents I care more about people and love than money and greed.

Parents I would not harm anyone without a reason.

My friends are my second family and my treasure.

My heart is bigger than most.

My truth is mine and I won't be sorry for the man I am today.

Do you ever question if the influence you had upon me was a fair one.

Do you ever question if you gave me enough love and affection.

I believe you did the best you could and learned from your mistakes.

I believe you had my best interest always at heart.

I am the man I wish to be, and I hope you feel connected to me for me.

Parents I know my life is lived different from your expectations of me at times.

A child is of his own individual making, to the person they become.

Parents I know you wanted to mould me into a little version of you.

I know as a parent it's just to see the best for me.

Parents I hope you take time to see.

I may not be always in line or flawless in my life.

One thing I can honestly say, you made a good man out of me.

I can honestly say, I love the version of me I've become.

All because of wisdom from you both.

All I am and all I will be.

Is thanks to you.

Thank You for the Sunshine

This life can bring you to the edge of nowhere.

Life can hide away our deepest secrets, our deepest dreams.

Leaving us lost in a cave where no light can shine through.

Rocks so heavy, I believed no matter how strong love may try, nothing will break into this cave of mine.

I miss seeing lights reflect off my face, I miss the heat of the sun.

I miss the warmth of someone to show me the sunshine above me.

In my cave, I feel all my love for life drain away into the shadows.

In the cave I became used to misery and despair.

In this cave, no love can exist in such a dark place with any light to shine in.

Then someone made of such light and love, broke down the rocks trapping me in darkness.

This someone came in and so did the light to follow and shine bright in a place spending years in the dark.

Thank you for the sunshine, thank you for showing me freedom from my own cell.

Thank you for the sunshine, it lights up every emotion in me, every desire set free.

Now I see roses grow and weeds die away.

Now I see rainbows and sunlight, not thunder in the sky.

Thank you for giving me a place to start over and thanks for giving me a way back.

I see balance in light and in dark, as before all my lights had went out.

Thanks to you all is beautiful, landscapes fresh and new.

I fell over the edge for a while, fell into a pile and could not see the good in anything around me.

I fell over the edge and was frozen in pain, time felt it had come to a standstill.

Thanks to beautiful people we have in life, we can overcome whatever barriers life sets in our way.

Now I'm recovering from living in a cave with no light.

Now I'm recovering from all that pulled me down into nothingness.

In recovering from this, I now see that having sunshine back is the key to a better version of reality.

Thank you for giving me my life back to see, to see I'm worth everything to everyone I love.

I lost my way, lost my track and felt no way of return from such a deep prison of my own making.

Your love and light showed me a way back, a way to see the sunshine in my life.

A way to live now where light is brighter than before all went dark on me long ago.

Thank you for this new lease of life, thank you for the sunshine back and thanks for the sunrise in my eyes once more.

Falling

In the moments we meet, I fall under your spell.

In the affections of your arms, your every embrace sends me falling.

Losing my sense of balance, falling into your world.

Falling into tonight, you gave me total pleasure, total excitement.

Falling with no warning, into the unknown, into each other's world.

Looking into your eyes, I see your soul, I feel safe.

You melt away all my worries, all my pain with one touch.

Falling for every word you speak.

Falling for each sunset with you.

Falling into a million stars with you.

Time gets lost in your company and each embrace we take.

I'm falling into you, falling unable to see any ground, any sense of this fall stopping.

Each day our connection begins to magnify into so much more than yesterday.

You melt away my worries, you melt away all that used to hurt me.

You drift into the night next to me.

As I lose my sense of reality in this life of real fantasy.

As I lose sight of how I used to live, and live more free in your company.

As we both fall into endless possibility, an unknown land.

The rush of this is electric, undeniable chemistry.

I continue to fall, and no sign of stopping or landing on solid ground.

I feel safe in falling into your world and falling into each other's lives.

Falling into you is something I feel we were meant to both do.

I feel as we look through our eyes, we share both of our worlds with equal passion, beautifully love affair

I feel I will fall forever and never land in a place of contentment.

I feel this fall will be eternal and I feel its taken place before.

This fall, this love, this fate of us.

This fall is into nowhere, yet we are discovering everywhere.

We discover more and more as we both continue to fall.

I Hope You Know

I was lucky to land in your path.
My heart beat fast on our first connection.
Seeing you entertain all you share talks with, makes me
      want you more.
I grow to love your light and you're dark.
I hope you see I look at you with pride and sparkle in
      my eye.
I love your humour and your style.
I love how your views open up my eyes to something
      new.
What I lack I find in you, and what you lack I give to
      you.
We learn from our love how to challenge each other's
      lives for the better.
I hope you know you're my soul mate, my destiny, my
      fate.
I express myself in all that I do, something not very
      natural to you.
You can escape danger with just some spoken words.
Between us both a team made unbeatable.
Betwccn us buth a bond undeniable.
I hope you know I thank you each day, you came my
      way.
I would lay down my life for you.
In all things we do, all things we share, you're my
      biggest lesson.
You keep me learning each day, how to love you in
      different ways.
I hope you know, my life had purpose, but with you it
      also has meaning.
You're my missing link, my other part of me.
I treasure you and all we have beyond any measure.
I hope you know, my heart is yours forever.

One Day Will Be Our Moment

I meet you and this was not our time to fall in love.
Your heart already lived in someone else's world.
I look in your eyes and the flames burn me up inside.
The chemistry between us electric, every touch wakes the senses.
We spend hours talking till the sun had finally fallen.
So much laughter in every day we shared, then you went home to your lover.
I wish my heart was yours and not shared between two places.
In the eyes of your lover I must keep us secret to protect you and I.
Seeing your lover treat you with no love or affection.
Seeing him not care at all about you, you appear invisible to his heart.
Your voice often unheard and valued very little.
Each stolen moment we take, feels like no mistake.
I feel no shame, as your lover had many chances to prove his love to you.
I hope soon you take the next step and see the love I have for you is much more true.
I feel time speed up every time we are together.
I feel time slow down when we are apart.
One day will be our moment that will set us both free.
Free from hidden encounters, free from stolen moments.
I hope one day I'm the only man to fill your heart and show you the world.
I believe in us meeting was meant to lead onto love.
I believe in soul mates, I believe it's you and I.
I see a sparkle in your eye every look you give me.
I am patient and will wait for you to decide on if I'm the one you wish to share yourself with.
Unrequited love is the cruelty I must face with each night I face without us coming together.

I live in the crime of knowing, this affair is deeper than just one night of passion.

The crime that we both commit every night we share together in each other's arms.

You live in a place of no love, no life and no compassion.

Once you free yourself from the prison you live in.

When you take the brave move to walk out and go it alone.

I will be here, I don't want any rush or confusion between us.

I want you to have space to breathe and space to let go of the one you once held dear.

I will be part of you, I will share what time you wish of me.

I will wait till the time is decided that me and you are right.

You're beautiful in every way that my imagination could hope for.

You're worth the wait, your wait, my time.

I will show you what real love devotion looks like

Passions of Us

Each new day waking up to you is a gift beyond all measure.
In the past I was hidden away from the world.
Never seeing all the beauty life had to offer.
Then I came across you and life opened up to wonder.
You held every part of my life in a fragile way.
My body was given affection never felt before now.
Our passion grows and leads down the same road together.
The passion of us is a melting of two hearts into one.
With you and I, we see adventures in the sky.
With you and I we travel to places, exploring many new spaces.
You have a beautiful way of seeing everything around us.
In your presence I feel safe, I feel free.
I feel like I'm in a state of mind of that of pure happiness, pure mystery.
All my years of loving, and losing.
All the years of storms and thunder, now rainbows light the way.
You have shown me how passionate love can be.
You have shown me how to live with no regret.
You have shown me how to throw away all my past and live for now.
I feel alive around you, like me and you belong.
Before you, I must have not been living, just breathing without feeling.
Your enlightenment by every experience you show me.
Your enlightenment by every touch you give me.
Before the passion of us, I must have just been dead inside but unaware.
The moment we have distance apart, I still feel your energy.

Miles may separate us from time to time.

Yet once we reconnect us, no time has passed.

We just pick up from yesterday, and carry on living
with each other for all that lies ahead of us.

With you I feel eternal bond, a light that will never
fade.

The passion of us, is here, and it's here forever more.

Different Versions of You and I

I fell into you and came to love you in every version of
you.

Sometimes you showed me you could be selfish and
have a heart of greed.

Sometimes you showed me how to see many sides to
life.

You told me life is not always fair, you told me life can
destroy us at any time.

Sometimes I showed you I could tell lies, and hide part
of me from you.

Sometimes I showed you beauty in all things can be
found.

In all different versions of you and me we come
together and belong to one other.

All the versions of you I adore, I love your
imperfections.

All of the versions of you keep turning and I see more
and more.

Every day I learn more of you and the mystery keeps
me in a state of fantasy.

I see the world through my eyes, you see the world in
your very own way.

No two eyes see the same view, no one sees life the
same way.

Our different versions of us, attracts us together in a
state of wonder.

I find you take me on adventures of the soul and of my
heart.

I find I take you on a journey of learning what love is,
when we act with a selfish heart.

You became softer and more willing to show you care,
by learning from my emotions.

I became harder by you showing me how to let emotion
be in my control.

I see different versions of you and I in every day we
share.

I never feel like any day will be the same, with you and
I it's always a brand new day than that of yesterday.

I believe in love seeing through life in different ways, is
a way to learn more about each other's heart.

I value no possessions, I find money has no importance
but just something we use to survive.

I value the life of the ones I love more than anything
else in life or any gain I could possess.

You seem to seek adventure in seeing the world and
wish to experience every emotion.

You seem to hold your values differently to that of
mine in some respects.

One thing that bonds us is our respect for each other's
way of living.

We share so much time together, and we spend time on
our own individual lives.

You have an eye for creative art and paint to express
yourself to the world.

I have my words and a pen to express my view on
every wonder I see, everything that I feel inside of
me.

Between both of our different versions of you and I.

We come together as one and blend and flow so
naturally as one.

We also remain unique to who we are and who we wish
to become.

This journey we started many years ago, it shows it's
always in a state of change and learning.

This journey I take with you I regret nothing and
treasure everything we have seen.

Conversation between us never seems to not flow or
have no new way to go.

Different versions of you and I are always changing,
but we have a natural way of sharing it so.

In every version of you and every version of me, I wish to share this all of my days with you and me.

Different versions of you and I have a direction that leads down the same road together.

We may see through different eyes, yet we blend as one and remain as two unique people.

You're the half of me I seek that makes me feel whole and complete.

Our two different versions of each other, fuse together by electric chemistry that no one can deny.

You and me are meant to be, this connection unbreakable and has stood the test of time.

You are the one I wish to share every night with, and see every sunrise in your arms.

My life is devoted to this bond we share, and I know you devote every thing to loving me too.

I forever will learn from you, and you from me.

My soul mate, my lover, my best companion in this life forever.

Mistake of Keeping Love Too Long.

Sometimes we fall for the greatest of mistakes.
My heart was blind to you, my mind fooled by you.
You chased me then you tossed me aside.
I fell from the mountain top with you to the sea below.
You lead me to believe I was everything to you.
Yet I feel like your friend not a lover to you.
You hide me from the world, you hide me inside a
cage.
We don't share life, I share a version of death with you.
Sometimes we fall for the greatest mistake.
The lesson that love can be meaningless.
We fall for a heart that beats only for its selfishness.
A heart unable to give back the affection it receives.
Sometimes we fall for the greatest mistakes.
We allow love to be given in such low quality.
We allow love with lack of passion to live in our hearts.
The greatest mistake is being so blind in love that left
so long ago.
Love that leaves us blind to see that so much more
beauty lays elsewhere.
Now I see love found in the right place can open the
mind to adventure.
Now I see love with you, left my heart long ago.
I deserve as do you to be happy once more.
We fall for the greatest mistake of allowing love that
died to live on in our life.
The greatest mistake believing we can't have what our
heart is seeking.
Believe in love and believe in yourself.
The best thing you can do is free your heart from an
unloved land.
I create new ways to get love wrong, to get my heart
torn up.

I see my heart is telling me to learn, to move on from you.

You're my greatest mistake, my greatest lesson, I loved you with all I have.

You took all of me, but gave me less of your heart over time.

I felt valuable in loving you.

The greatest mistake we can fall for is our hearts misleading guide to love.

The best way to live is to accept all the bad happens to shape us.

The best way to live is to see all experience is given for us to see different views.

The key to the greatest mistake in love is to not accept when it's time for goodbye.

Goodbye can be uplifting, can let us see, different versions of love out there.

So much more love to feel, love that matches our heart's desires.

Learn from the greatest mistake of loving past its sell by date.

Walk away from hurt, walk away and let yourself be free to let real love come your way.

Learn from your biggest mistakes in love and fall for a heart that's pure and open.

Fall into the arms of someone willing to love, it can be found in places unexpected.

In places we don't expect to find, love can be pure if two hearts join as one.

Love can be intoxicating if two twin souls meet.

The greatest lesson is to know when to leave love and when to arrive in new love.

Don't fear an exit in a goodbye.

Don't fear an introduction into some new land.

Love can be the greatest thing you can feel, when two twin minds and hearts meet.

I've learned from my greatest mistake, and left it all
    behind me.
Now all I see is the future in my eyes as the past is
    nothing but a final goodbye.

Learn to Breathe

All I see you do is rush and tear.
Not stopping for a moment to care.
Your heart beats faster than a blink
Inside of you is thunder and rage.
Each hug I give I sense fear and sadness.
Let me tell you some wisdom.
I don't worry how high I climb
I don't compare my life to anyone.
I relax when my work is done.
Life is no race to win.
Life without freedom, and friends, holds no value in
    the end.
Learn to breathe, learn to slow down and see all beauty
    in life.
Give yourself love, give yourself joy.
Life is not for winners, life is not for greed.
Life you should relearn how to breathe.
Take time to slow down your pace, breathe and see.
Life is a wonderful adventure if you take it all in.
If you run the pace you do, all will be a blur.
If you live this way, you will miss out on fun.
Learn to slow down, learn to breathe.
See life from a new point of view.
Less chaos and stress in your mind.
Less demands on your time, means that you will see.
What truly matters when you learn to slow down and
    just breathe.

Since I Found You.

All of my life I felt I was looking for a new way of
living.

Life had every day on repeat, nothing was a surprise to
me.

Love had left me and my life fell apart for a while.

Then one day by chance you came my way.

You had a smile that was infectious, you had a touch
electric.

Your passion for living, your ambition was fearless.

You made me feel alive, you put the fire back in my
eyes.

You picked me up, shock me up and made me believe
impossible was just a point of view.

We talked and we talked, hours would pass unnoticed
at all.

Since I found you my drive to live races faster every
day we share.

Since I found you, no day feels predictable.

We rumble around and play in the sun.

We laugh every day we spend together, no day is now
a repeat of yesterday.

With us, every day is brand new and has such different
views to take in.

With you everything makes sense, you lift me up and
boost my confidence.

With you I feel respect for all of me, you truly make me
feel accepted for all that I am.

I don't feel I need to alter me to a version you could
love.

You love that I have imperfections and you treasure
them so.

Since I found you, I ask myself what makes me the
lucky one to have you fall in love with me.

I wish to lay my life down for you and share my everything.

I intend to devote my heart to seeing what you wish life to blossom into between us.

Since you came into my life, all I see is colours and all I hear in my head is beautiful music.

All that once was a sense of doubt to me that love is never possible to find and almost never lasts.

Now you and I bounded and I walk on the clouds and feel air beneath each step we take.

You're the other half of my life, you and I have many memories of falling in love and many more memories to dream of and then create.

Since I found you, you found me this light between our two worlds burns bright for all to see.

You're a star that I finally found, you're the treasure nothing can place a value upon.

Now I live not just for me, I live to learn how to love you better each day we enter in together.

All I want to do is show you many ways in which to smile, many versions of happiness can be found.

My eyes opened up to love again the day you came my way.

Thank You

One day out of fate we crossed paths.

My mind was seeking someone unique to start a new adventure.

Days and years of love and lessons learned before you came my way.

This new love affair turned both our worlds inside out.

Years passed, and love with you made me grow and alter into someone kinder than before.

You made me became so much stronger just in your presence, an energy like no other.

You showed me how to see the sun, even when it rains.

You showed me how to walk away from hate, to let only love in.

You and I grew in new directions as the years passed.

You and I ended on a positive memory of this love affair.

You loved me with good intentions, you connected to my soul.

Thank you for loving me for the man I am, for giving me all you can.

Thanks for all the memories I will always treasure.

I learned how love can be through your undeniable affection you gave.

Thanks for seeing past my flaws, for seeing my light and supporting my dark.

I believe we were given these years to love and move on.

You were a chapter of my life, a lesson in love and in myself I had to learn.

No anger or regret exists in me from us coming to the end of this journey started so long ago

Thank you for this experience in life and in matters of the heart.

Thank you for giving me all of you and letting me in
your heart
Thank you

Different Versions of the Lonely

We all get lonely sometimes, a sense of disconnect.
The days as a young boy, in a playground full of kids.
Yet I felt invisible, I felt not able to touch reality.
I felt I was invisible energy, like a ghost unable to talk
to the living.
Then we can feel lonely in a room full of our family.
Our unique being can be seen as too individual, too
brave.
I often felt like I was lonely in my family affairs.
We can all have different versions of what lonely can
be.
Alone in work, doing the nine to five no one aware of
our presence.
Alone in a relationship where sharing a life with
someone becomes a silent room
Alone in our own company unable to feel love for our
own time to be who we wish to be.
Different versions of lonely exist in so many ways.
I believe to be alone and not feel lonely is the key.
I believe in being loved for all you are can be found.
I believe if we settle for loneliness we are saying our
self worth is less valued than others.
Everyone deserves to feel a sense of love, a sense of
passion and adventure.
Everyone deserves to feel a connection to people in our
lives., connection to this life we all share.
If you see a lonely heart, give them some notice, give
them conversation.
You may just awaken a beautiful mind, a beautiful
person who lost their way some time ago.
Confidence to change from loneliness to a version of
themselves forgotten.
All you lonely people, believe in your individuality.

All you lost and lonely, seek minds that see how much resides in your beautiful mind.

Most experience a different version of being lonely sometimes.

Most can experience a sense of rejection in a room that's full.

Different versions of lonely will leave the heart to spill empty.

The ways to not be lonely can be yours.

Anyone you feel a connect to, don't deny yourself what the journey will be.

Every connection made, will grow your heart into something stronger.

The more you let go of fear, fear in what others may see.

The more you will be a version of you that will attract a life full of wonder.

Be free, be you, be brave, be individual.

Be a version of you that leads to a version of you that feels lonely no more.

We all experience different versions of loneliness.

We all sometimes have different versions of loneliness .

The key is to learn how to feel whole in loving you.

The key to break free from all versions of loneliness you may feel.

Let go of the rules you hide behind and live once more free from all versions of loneliness.

If The Mind Ruled The Heart

We fall in love, from the heart's connection.

While we try and discover where the heart is leading us.

The heart driven by emotion, defying all logic of the mind.

What if we lived not through the heart but the mind.

Unable to feel the rush and spark of chemistry connections.

A world where our love was logic and robotic, no feelings.

So the mind would only allow us to match up with others of the same intelligence.

We would stop learning from the mistakes love has to teach.

We would stop feeling butterflies in such a rush of passion and adventure of the foolish heart's affairs.

In the world where the mind was ruling the heart.

I imagine we would all live sharing someone based on data, based on background, based on the perfect match in the eyes of the mind.

In a world where the mind ruled the heart we would never fall in love anymore.

We would only view our interactions with others through logic, void of emotion.

No more passion, no more falling in love.

At best you would feel safe in your surroundings.

In a world where the heart was ruled by the head.

No one would fall in love.

No one would moan the loss of your passing.

No one would feel strong enough to protect you from harm.

No one would lift you up when the world pulls you down.

No one would care about your experiences in life.

No one would rescue anyone from anything.

In truth I believe, we may say don't let your heart rule your head.

In reality it would be a world void of love if the mind was to rule the head instead.

So I feel I live, love and grow, by my heart ruling my head.

I could not live in a world where the mind ruled the heart instead.

Leaving all emotion to die, all logic life.

To me the heart is designed to rule our heads.

The heart will always show us so much joy.

The heart will let us make foolish mistakes in love.

I don't regret any moments, any love, and any lessons.

All from my heart ruling my head.

Echoes in the Atmosphere

We all have dreams, we all have fantasies in our mind.

I've placed coins in many wishing wells to make my dreams heard.

In silence, in our head we wish upon a coin and hope.

Hope someone hears our heart's desires.

Little do we all know, our wishes do get heard.

As the penny falls to the bottom of the wishing well.

As we make our wish in our mind.

It sends echoes into the atmosphere.

Forces and angels living in the atmosphere hear our inner voice, and wishes.

Angels living in the atmosphere lead us to places so our wishes can come true.

Angels send us signs, angels speak to our minds.

For those of us turned into the invisible world of angel light.

We find ourselves in places, situations where our dreams seem to take place.

We think our wishes don't get heard by anyone apart from our own mind

Little do you know the wish in the wishing well gets sent like echoes in the atmosphere.

So next time you have a wish come true.

Remember that wishes get sent and heard by angels that live with and protect us.

Angles that listen to the echoes in the atmosphere.

Divine intervention, from angels living in the atmosphere

LIGHT

In life we come across pure hearts sometimes.

When you guided me, I felt your honest heart.

You have no bad intentions and give all you can.

I looked up to you and wished to learn from your wisdom.

You amazed me by your motivation to do well by everyone.

You amazed me by your sense of self worth.

You are made of pure white light.

Your light destroys all the dark in the room.

When you enter a room your present is uplifting.

Light hearted lady, you amaze me with your spirit.

You care about everyone a pure way.

You hold onto values even when others do not.

Anyone accepted in your light , you must value.

You only shine brighter on the ones that truly make you smile.

Your energy is undeniable.

Your light is your greatest gift .

You light every one with your touch.

Light hearted lady I respect you so much.

White light guides you to always be kind, honest, and true.

Destiny of a Mum to Be

Destiny of a mum to be.
You've always had and held the key.
The challenges of a long career.
At times you felt a puzzle piece was missing.
Kept walls up and around your heart.
Now as a mum to be, the walls have broken and the heart runs completely free.
Loving new fragile life, under your very protection.
Having your eyes look in all directions.
Destiny of a mum to be, the most important role you will ever hold.
When you are lost, look inside for instincts to guide you.
One day this person will look at you and smile.
As you I know will be an ace and loving mum.
All you have learned, is nothing to compare to this new chapter.
You will be the mum you were meant to be.
You have always had and held the key, to be a mum was in your destiny.

Black Roses

I had a life of love and wonder when we came into each
other's world.
My heart devoted to opening up your life to a unique
kind of love.
Then I discovered so much more to me, by allowing
your love in.
We used to share such colour in our conversation, then
I hit a wall.
As I fell, you walked away from my bleeding heart.
You left me to recover without my lover, my best
friend.
It was never lack of love you held in your heart for me.
It was lack of empathy, and escaping from my issues.
You loved me at my highest, and dropped me at my
lowest.
You are not full of colour, you're pulling me into dark
places.
You're telling me one story, but clearly you have two
faces.
The one you show me, and your face of deception for
everyone else you hold dear.
Red roses are beauty, and light up a room.
You once were my red rose, then over time you turned
black.
Black rose man, you're lost in some lonely land
A place where you are distant and cold.
Black rose man, I hope you find a way back.
Back from doom, back to the man I once loved.
The man in the mirror today, is a pale shade of grey.
You need to embrace your heart again, embrace your
light.
Black rose man, I hope you have a way to learn to let
hate go.

Black rose man, I hope you learn to love yourself
again.

Black rose man, please come back in the sun.

I hope in all we once shared.

You have no regrets, no need to apologize.

We headed into directions that became non parallel.

We lost a connection as the chemistry stopped in its
tracks.

Black roses if given love will fade to colour and beauty.

I must say goodbye, I will never share my life with you
again.

With all that said and done, I'm thankful for our time
together

You once shared beautiful colour conversations with
me.

Now I see you're turning the black roses back to red.

I hope you're never misled by your negative mind.

One day I wish you find peace in everyone, and
everything you do.

A lover should be your friend till the end, and never
judge you by your front cover.

Black rose man, come back, be the man I know you can

Electricity

You talked to me, made me feel a spark, a touch electric.

Chemistry between our minds caused electric fusion.

Your eyes tell me you're alive, with power and drive.

I sense your energy is built up inside.

All your emotions held inside, explosion overdue.

You have never felt chemistry with such passion before.

You felt no connection and love worth the fight.

I awaken your senses and spark your adventure.

I drive your imagination wild, with my plans for us.

Our electricity causes lights to flicker and dim.

I spark your interest, awareness for endless possibility.

You also show me life has so much beauty.

New versions of reality I'm yet to uncover with you and me.

Electricity speeds around my body faster in your presence.

Electricity is between us, I won't question this connection.

Electricity that drives two hearts to beat as one, is something rare to see.

With us I feel in sync with you, electric heartbeats.

You're what I've longed to seek in love.

You're my spark that lights up my flames.

Endless paths we've yet to take together.

Endless experiences to yet see and discover.

That our power of attraction, electricity, is forever till the lights go out on us both.

Hell is Where You Left Me

I fell for you, what else was I meant to do.

You put on a show, and I sat in the front row.

You made me believe you were the one to be my all.

Then one day you betrayed me in every way a man possibly can.

You stole all from me, you made everyone take your side.

You infect others with your poison and left me high and dry.

You walked away, when I needed you the most.

All I can say is what did you expect from me.

I did my best to show you I'm worth all your time.

You stayed away, I lost my sight of every part of me.

Hell is where you left me, and I handled it all alone

Hell is where I stayed and the devil talked to me.

He made sense, told me to show you what I'm made of.

Show you how it feels, revamp of me I started to do.

Reinvented all of my life, climbed out of hell where you left me to be.

Now I'm on the other side, I'm back on top and in control.

You were the first thing I let go, I won't take your lies anymore.

I won't stay from a distance and be a puppet you master and expect me to obey.

Darling you cast me aside, I was the one you said you loved more than anything.

You're weak as you have infected everyone with poison.

To be honest I don't want to surround myself by toxic people and loveless souls.

Hell is where you left me, when I had lost my mind and fallen apart.

You think you're so above learning, you're not able to love with a strong heart.

True love is when you fight the corner for the one you adore, you just let others attack me and break me.

Hell is where you left me, the moment you walked away..

I thought it was me to blame, I thought I was full of so much shame.

I regret the final moments we shared, the moment you left me in my hour of need.

Hell is where you left me, I thought it was all me.

I have woken up, seen the light for all that it is.

I broke free from hell, where you left me the day I walked out on you and all your games.

You may not say much, but your intentions were not as pure as I thought.

Hell is where you left me, but I live there no more.

I live for all of me, I believe in love after a death of a heart.

I don't regret loving you for so much good times were shared.

I just felt hurt and rejected the day you left me in hell to escape all alone.

One thing I am is a fighter, one thing I am is stronger than most.

I learned a lot since I left you, I've reflected and I see who I am.

I see I'm worth so much more than what you had to offer, I am worth my dark and my light.

You love and adored my light and all I had to give to you.

You took more than you gave in return, I believe you loved me the best way you could.

Only thing is I'm worth handling at my worst hour, and seeing the storm through.

You took the good, could not handle the dark.

Now I'm out all alone, my smile back and a bounce in
every step.

You lost me the day you left me in hell all alone with
no way out, leaving me to battle alone.

You're not worth my tears, you're not worth any more
fights any more of my time.

I will love someone who loves my dark and also my
light.

You and I Were Not Meant to Be.

The day arrived, you took your bags and left this home
   we once shared.
I let you go, I felt it was best this way.
All the fighting left me feeling nothing but empty for us
   and empty inside this home.
As you close the door, I felt a sense of release a sense
   this was not meant to be any longer.
I felt tears flow down my cheeks, not of sadness but of
   release.
I felt afraid of starting over, but with you it was lonely
   and lifeless.
I lived life through all your plans, and followed all your
   demands.
I dusted off my low self esteem, I polished up my
   confidence.
I made life worth living, I was alone but not lonely.
With you the house where you and I once lived felt
   empty.
I reinvented my home and made every room my own.
I closed every door that led back to you.
I felt warm inside, excited for life ahead.
You never loved me, you just made me feel like a token
   man.
You felt you could buy my affection, buy my heart.
My heart was never for sale, my affections priceless.
One night you showed up wanting me back.
You had a great story to tell, it would have been a best
   seller.
Yet you don't fool me any more, you won't be coming
   through any door that leads back to me.
You were a master of deception, told many versions of
   yourself.
You wanted someone to follow you, bow down and see
   life from only your point of view.

Darling I bow down to no man, I almost fell in love with you.

I surrendered my heart, and you tortured it so.

I surrendered my life and you only adored yourself.

You were my lesson, you made me see that true love is worth seeking.

Love that is equal, love that two people share.

You and I were not meant forever, just a chapter in each other's life.

I learned that I can't love someone who adores himself more than anyone else.

I hope you see from your lonely land, that if you love you too much.

You will never feel what true love is, and what it can be to two hearts.

Now I see only me, and I wait for love to find me.

Now I see clear, I see with new eyes and I'm free.

I seek my equal, I seek a heart that is open.

I seek someone with a gentle heart, until that day I will live life my way.

You and I were not meant to be, but I believe someone out there is meant for me.

I believe in love, I never will give up on my fairy tale ending and my prince to seek me out.

Now for my life to carry on ascending higher, so I see from a higher view.

That somewhere down there is a man meant just for me and me meant just for him.

Love Makes Us Act Like Fools

Love is cruel, it makes the wisest of men and women act like fools.

The need to be seen always at our best, to put on a show to impress.

Then along comes unrequited love affairs, the ones that never reply to our desires.

Loving the ones already taken, and painfully we watch from afar.

Loving the ones that we feel are not in a league we can touch.

Having put up the one we desire to a status of a god and not a mortal.

How can we possibly get the affections of those we put above us and not on an equal playing ground.

Beauty also is cruel in love, the ones we fall for and feel our looks make us unnoticed by so many.

Love is about our connections to someone else's mind and all a matter of chemistry we can't define.

We can't explain why we fall in love with the people we come to share our life with.

Attraction is in a law of its own, and the rules always changing and updating.

So how do any two lovers ever get to share the journey and never fall apart.

All because we take the risk each day, to behave like fools and flirt our way into the eye of our attention.

All because we may have lost love, fallen out of love and yet we continue to play the game.

We may say we don't play games, we are better than that and yet every love affair has a push and a pull.

Sometimes you have the power and you pull all the stings and your lover follows your lead.

Sometimes they push you back unexpectedly and we fall back down and they retake the power.

In true love, this effect of push and pull is always
taking place.

It's the beauty of falling in love, acting like fools, and
always in a cat and dog race.

Sometimes you're the dog chasing the cat, beware and
don't be fooled as sometimes the cat chases back.

This game we all seem to play in love, it is very
different between every two connections made.

When two people burn the same flame, love can be an
interesting eternal love game.

Foolish Hearts

One more time, tell me why you act in such foolish
    ways, heart of mine
Why you give so much love away, in such rush of lust
    and desire.
I came into your life and walked your affections into
    new fantasies.
I showed you a taste of what could be our reality.
Then I fell into your web of entrapment, your lair of
    lies.
Foolish heart you walk into love so blind to see.
When your new lover is using you to pass the time and
    nothing deeper..
Foolish heart, don't fall for this crime and open your
    eyes.
Foolish heart even beautiful people tell incredible lies
    to get closer to parts of you.
Foolish heart why don't you teach me, to see through
    eyes of deception.
Foolish heart you give me no protection.
In all the fires set off in my heart, I put them out, dust
    myself down and try and love again.
Foolish heart I don't wish to play all these games.
Foolish heart when will you wise up, wake up and be
    aware.
Be aware when love is nothing more than an illusion in
    clever mastered conversation.
Foolish heart I can't always take your advice, matters of
    finding my true lover's existence.
As you allow me to make such foolish love mistakes.
The one thing I feel through all the lovers that have
    come and gone.
Is love is worth something to spend time to seek.
Even if you foolish heart make me so valuable and
    weak.

Valuable to falling for many different versions of being loved.

Valuable to being hurt in many different places, many different ways but different faces.

Weak to not see when my foolish heart walks into love so blind, so fast.

Unable to see the difference between a gem and a slab of dark emotion and no love to give.

Foolish heart I may have suffered so much joy from many lovers in my lifetime.

Foolish heart I don't regret all the mistakes you lead me to learn, when I was left in flames when love would burn.

Foolish heart I will continue to seek out love, seek out my equal to share every part of me.

Foolish heart one day, I will look back on all this and say.

Foolish heart, you made me so much wiser, so much kinder and so much more real.

Foolish heart without all the places we went together, I would have never seen so much.

Foolish heart you have taught me so much about different versions of love.

Foolish heart you're part of me, and foolish heart I am sure to always be.

In a place of seeking love, in many different foolish ways.

One day I will be a wise heart, make smarter choices in my life.

Till that day arrives I remain in a close relationship with my foolish heart and I.

Foolish heart I will stay on this road of unknown love affairs.

One day, this heart of mine will be wiser and see, the love that's meant for me.

Foolish heart you give me so many lessons, so many directions I could take.

Foolish heart, love is always going to be a game, sometimes we win, and sometimes we lose.

Most of all, we carry on seeking the heart meant to beat in sync with our own.

Foolish heart lays in all of us, till we learn to have the love in a form we seek.

Love designed for me, individual and hand crafted and meant to be.

Cages

I feel in love with you, unaware of your intentions to never care.

Freedom was mine, then you lead me down a path with your deception.

I had many walls around me, you made me feel safe and take my guard away.

Over time small chains started to form around the walls of my heart.

Small chains dragging me down from confidence to a land of no respect.

I feel for your intentions, I feel for your mind games and tricky ways.

I did my best to escape and run away once I saw love was not in your plan.

You wanted a puppet to be under your control, leaving me feeling lost and alone.

My flaws you would magnify, leaving me question my worth to anyone else if I left you.

My heart of gold you left out in the rain to rust and crumble away.

Over time I felt the chains grow much more heavy on my heart.

In my life with you, I came to feel chained down and in a cage under lock and key.

You give me limited freedom to be me.

You took away my independence, and shattered all my confidence.

You made me feel my individuality was only loveable by you.

You would highlight all my mistakes and never be proud of my achievements I had made.

In this cage I live, I live for only you.

In this cage, we only have each other, you would share no one with my company.

My energy began to drain and my heart felt empty from years of loneliness.

I know I had to escape your chains and cage, start a life without you.

My tears started to fall, the day I would imagine this life could be my fate if I let it.

So I decided to leave, and break your chains and free myself from your cage.

The day I left, my heart felt light come back in.

Love is about an equal not someone to place in chains and tell them how to behave.

Love is about having trust to give freedom, love is something that should lift you up.

I see the lights now, I feel my heart beat with love once more.

This love is for myself, and knowing I'm worth so much more.

Yesterday's Heart Seems So Far Away

I held onto love with you long after we parted.

I remember the long night conversations, you shared your wisdom with me.

So young, so unaware of how life can change our path.

You left life far too young, you left scars on my heart.

I would give anything to share another day with you.

I have a strength that you showed me, a confidence you gave me.

Yesterday's heart seems so far away.

Only yesterday we talked and shared so much joy.

My heart will always love you, and my heart lives in yesterday.

I need to live in the present, but my memories are of yesterdays with you.

You were my biggest aspiration, my biggest devotion was to you.

You were my best friend in life, and even now you're gone.

Yesterday's heart and memories for you, lives on in me.

I feel part of you lives in my heart.

I feel a sense of strength like never before.

I feel your protection still even after your leaving this world.

You were my mum, my friend, my guide, my life.

Yesterday's heart may seem so far in the distance as time passes by.

But in my memories you will always remain alive.

I still hear your wisdom, I still feel you close.

Yesterday was painful and I was trapped in sadness.

Now I feel able to say, I feel you in me and I will join you one day.

Look over me as I live my life, I will make you proud mum that I was your son.

Yesterday's heart you are far away, but I'm now in the
  present.
In the present I accept my mum is somewhere new.
In the present I accept you passing onto some other life.
In my memories you will remain until my dying day.
In my heart you continue to grow even though your
  soul is elsewhere.
Your light, your love, your energy lives somewhere
  much more full of beauty.
You live somewhere that matches your light.
Somewhere else where you can shine.
Just as bright.

Pretty Lady

Pretty lady lead life your own way.
Look at the wishes you make at night.
Face all that comes with grace and a slow steady pace.
Take all your mistakes and turn them into lessons.
This world is not a fair one.
Your heart always warms a room.
Love is a gift that one day you will share with one man.
Pretty lady stay close to me, I will always be near.
Pretty lady share your dreams with me.
Pretty lady share your day with me.
Some men will steal your heart, leaving it empty.
Pretty lady let them leave, don't fight for the sake of
   love.
All the lies you have been told.
Promises of love.
Promise of a fairy tale ending.
This can all be yours one day.
But pretty lady let love come your way.
My friendship will protect you, my devotion shield
   you.
Pretty lady lead life your own way.
Trust your emotions, trust our friendship.
Pretty lady never change for anyone.
In the sunset a man will come your way, one day.

Price of Being Me

I have been torn into a millions pieces, broken over and over.

Watched the skies fall upon me, in quicksand I fall.

The price I paid for being individual was a high one.

Being true to my reflection caused me many scars along the way.

When you stand for something, often you stand alone.

Jealous minds everywhere prey on knocking successful people down.

Every one in any spotlight pays a price sometimes.

I found out the hard way, the price of being me cost me dearly.

Everyone out there stand for something, live true to your wishes.

I don't believe in taking a bow to be a conformist.

I believe in growing into your own skin comes from a light within.

We must battle through a forest of monsters to find the people with pure intentions.

I paid over and over for speaking my mind but I refuse to be put in a box and told how to behave.

All you unique minded individuals keep living and never conform to what the papers say.

Everyone out there who felt they must shy away from living.

I'm living proof that you can live any which way you damn well please.

I'm living proof you live outside the box and show the world you don't care.

I'm living proof that even after everyone set out to destroy me for me.

I have climbed the mountains, I have paid the price of being me.

It's all been worthwhile, as now I feel stronger, wiser and free.

I have the ones who love me for all that I am.

I have let go of everyone who set out to fool me, use me and abuse me.

Some people get satisfaction from destruction of those who live in harmony in their own skin.

All because they are restless and lost, they want to break me but they never will.

I would pay the price for being me over and over.

As paying that price I stayed true to following my very own star.

My star bright and strong for all those to see.

Everyone out there stay true to the life you wish to live.

Focus on the love that kind people share, cast aside hate and monsters into the sea.

I paid a price along the way to being the man I am today.

Would I pay that price again, I would pay it over and over.

As living for me and no one else is priceless and worth it, living for no one else but me.

Live for you and no one other set of rules, be happy and be free.

I would pay the price every time if it means living just for me.

Sorry For My Human Side

As a young man I didn't care as much on hurt I would dish out.
I would not listen to the wisdom of my parents' words.
I have told lies to protect myself from harm.
I've stolen from places and didn't see the crime
I've cheated on people with my heart.
Sorry for my human side.
Sorry it took me so long to learn.
I've let people down when I hide from everyone.
Sometimes I am not good to myself and neglect my life.
Sorry for my very human side.
I believe we all make mistakes in our lives.
I believe those who can't admit a flaw, tell the deepest of lies to themselves.
I've grown in my loyalty to the ones I love.
I don't steal from places I used to feel didn't matter.
I'm in love with my own life and have a new sense of being.
I treat those around me with kindness and compassion.
I've learned to be humble and treat life as a gift not a curse.
I'm still human, I never will be flawless in my life.
Yet I feel now I've grown into a better version of me.
I have no regrets and no more apologies to make.
As without my mistake, misguided roads.
I would not have turned into the man I'm proud to be today.
Sorry for my human side, my mistakes.
All mistakes have made me learn.
All mistakes have shaped my character today.
I'm me, I'm now heading towards the man I wish to become.

Dark Heart

It was not always this dark inside your heart, all the lights turned out.

You once lived in a place full of bright rays of sunshine.

Along the way hurt blocked out all the skies around you.

Your heart became heavy, it weighed you down.

Your heart faded to a deep shade of black.

Dark heart find a way back from this cave you're now in.

Dark heart I feel you falling into despair, far away from my love and affection.

You had love that left you, this has scarred your world and left you broken.

You can live in regret, you can be frozen in yesterday.

Please dark heart, love may have left you.

Love can be found in the strangest of places.

Dark heart, take this time on your own, to love yourself once more.

For so long, your identity was led through someone else.

For so long you had no individual self, you were controlled by love.

Over time I see you move on from this, you will love again.

My friendship is here dark heart, to help you see beauty in life once more.

All that hurts you, let it come to rest.

All the demons you allow to hunt your heart, find a way to release them.

I see a bright light slowly return to you as you heal and grow into someone new.

Someone who has finally moved on.

Light will enter your world soon, once the memories of
yesterday fade away.
Light will come back on, only then will you truly move
on.

Where Do Lost People Go?

Sometimes in life we get lost, nowhere wakes our flames.

We all are made from the roads walked upon.

My confused heart leads me in mixed directions.

We all have a purpose for our energy and light.

We all have something to do, some effect on our surroundings.

Forces beyond us direct and guide us.

Forces beyond us send us signals and messages.

Wasted years in a life of our choice, but fate has a plan in store.

Where do these lost people go, when nowhere feels like home.

Where do they lay their dreams too, when reality is distorted in view.

Lost people you have one key, one destination, one world.

Lost people are everywhere if you look close in the eyes of others.

Lost people take a moment of silence and block out all the noise.

Lost people once you awaken your identity, the rest will follow.

Lost people let go of too much control on finding your way.

The more you let go of forcing fate, the more you're open to let in the answers you seek.

Lost people you will end up where you need to be, just let go of your tight grip on destiny.

Lost people go with the unfolding of fate.

Lost people you will end up where you're meant to be.

Love is Not Demanding

I look into tomorrow as the sun falls on another day.

I look into the mirror's reflection of yesterday to see all the cracks.

I used to demand so much from love, expectations and demanding wishes.

My respect for you was low, I believed I was the only one allowed to speak and get heard.

I was to blame for the hurricane in this relationship.

I was to blame for allowing love to be demanding, love should be uplifting.

Crimes I committed on your heart will leave scars, scars will need to heal.

One day when you went to exit our life we shared.

I became aware of my mistakes, you gave me one chance to prove myself to you.

You told me love is not demanding it is something shared with an equal understanding.

Love is not meant to drain the heart of all it has to offer, but to fill it so it beats much faster.

Love is freedom of expressing a bond of unique connection.

Love is about eternal affection, eternal communication and romance should never die.

Love should never feel lonely, love should always continue to grow in the same direction.

No matter the differences we have, we must meet in the middle of a mutual respect.

I used to demand all of you, and give very little in return.

I would demand you never put yourself before me or anyone else.

Almost losing the greatest thing to come my way, gave me a reason to wake up today.

You have shown me I must have my individuality as so should you.

My life is my own, and so is yours.

I have learned that expectations of you were all to benefit my world.

I have learned you desire to feel the freedom to grow and change.

You're not something I have purchased in a shop, I don't have ownership over your life.

You're my lover, my other half of what I lack.

I have my ambition, my drive and direction to succeed.

Along the highway of my climb to somewhere I felt was more important than us.

I lost my eyes and vision to see, you're the best thing to ever happen to me.

Frankenstein's Heart Can't Beat for Someone Else.

We were young, carefree and had magic in the air around us.

We shared growing up together, we found love in each other.

My heart would beat in sync with you.

You promised to love me and me only eternal.

Right up till our dying day and life separates us from this world.

I saw you in all your beauty and viewed you from up close, I felt every heartbeat.

We shared time in many sunsets, many different lands.

We shared our life together, we had a plan in motion for our days ahead.

We devoted our hearts, lives, minds, and souls to one another

Nothing could have torn up our bond, nothing came between us.

One unexpected day, one tragic twist in my life with you.

You got taken, you died in my arms and I felt every fiber of my being go numb.

What could I live for, now you've gone onto some new plane of existence.

I felt lost, alone and afraid of what the future would hold.

I was driven mad by anger that life stole your heart from me.

I was driven by rage that life stole your beautiful body from under me.

I created Frankenstein to hold your mind and heart in.

I use electricity to bring you alive to be near me once more.

Creating a body to hear you speak once more to me.

This was the most selfish act I have ever done.

Frankenstein's heart won't beat in sync like we once did.

Frankenstein's body is only a vessel, nothing can replace holding you.

Frankenstein spoke and you had no clue who I was.

You sounded scared of the view and where you were.

No one should play god, it's not a power we can handle or master.

So I decided that I must go through the grief of losing my soul mate.

I turned off the machine, I didn't raise you up to live in a body not yours.

I'm sorry I almost created Frankenstein to live so you would never die.

I will continue this life without you for now.

One day I believe when it's my last heartbeat, my final hour.

I will travel as energy and transform to find you.

You're my soul mate, my eternal sunshine.

I will never lose my love for you, I will see you someday soon.

You were my light to my dark, my angel to my demons.

You loved me completely and took me for who I am, past. present and everything in-between.

You're my love of my life, you're my destiny in some day I will find and love you once more.

Black Holes and Shiny Rainbows

Sometimes we start falling into darkness.
With no reason we feel unprotected everywhere we go.
Lost in all that we try and do.
Unable to see reality, confusion taking over me.
Seeing black holes, falling into nothingness.
Looking for somewhere safe to land.
When no day seems to appear bright and clear.
No sunshine around, storms in the skies.
Feeling so low then extremely high.
Lost in black holes, looking for shiny rainbows.
Around me used to be lights and fantastic sounds.
Now all that hides underground.
In blackness we fall, feeling we have nothing at all.
We push away all the love we treasure.
Far into a distant land, no one left to understand.
Protecting others, while breaking my heart.
At the end of black holes, I look for shiny rainbows.
The bright lights, the excitement of knowing.
The light is somewhere glowing.
Lost in black holes looking for shiny rainbows.
So far in the dark, unable to see a way of escape.
Then one day, the black hole faded away.
Finally after years I'm free from the black holes I lived
   in.
I'm finally in a wonderland of shiny rainbows.

Angels of Protection

In the darkness, comes fear of the unknown future.
Someone feels close to me but yet unseen.
Someone I feel is coming for an intervention to this life.
I sense love in the dark, still only an energy I can feel but not touch.
Out of the shadow comes a stranger made of white light.
What does this mean, what do you want from me, stranger of the night.
Then you told me you're my guide, my angel of protection.
You have come to bring me away from this path I'm on.
I am your guide that watches over you each day.
Angels are not meant to be seen, just leave clues for us to find.
Angels that rebel to protect and lead us from harm.
Angels of protection arrive just in time.
White light that surrounds you, you place some light on me.
I then felt a sense of where I had gone wrong and where I need to be.
I looked around to speak to my guide to my heart's wrong choices.
Yet this angel of protection had already vanished from view.
We all lose sight of the way we should travel sometimes.
We all lose a sense of what we must do, and what makes us alive inside.
We all have a purpose, we all have a guide.
I will never forget the day I was touched by that white light and had my sense of worth returned.

I believe in each of us is a reason to being, and a way in which we all must live.

No one lives the same, no one feels any day the same way.

Now I have found I have my own purpose, my life filled with meaning.

Everyone's heart beats for a purpose, everyone has a role to play.

In life it's just a mystery, we all need to find our star to follow.

Everyone has a role to play, I learned mine the day my guide showed me the way.

Connect to the intention of your own heart and see, you have a reason in which to be.

Creative Hearts Must Suffer Sometimes to Create Art

Throughout my life, I felt inflections on my character.

Throughout my life I felt misunderstood by most.

Accepted by very few that could see past my mistakes and encourage my talent.

Often I lived a lie, trying to find the reason to my pointless life.

I was the unique child that everyone threw bricks at.

I was the teenager that followed my very own star.

Out of somewhere I found my imagination was mine to create and flow in any way I wished.

Cruelty came to me from having a mind of free will.

Cruelty comes when others sense you have life worked out.

I would take all the negative words thrown at me and make rainbows.

Creative hearts often suffer from life's wounds and tests.

Creative hearts must suffer to blossom art from pain.

Look behind the eyes of an artist and his beauty.

Look behind the heart of every creative soul.

You will see someone who had to suffer in the dark to produce beauty from grit and destruction of a life.

Creative hearts are made from broken pieces.

Creative hearts suffer sometimes, thanks to all the hurt I produce such beautiful art.

Thanks to all the pain, thanks to all those who made a choice to tear away at my heart.

Where are you now, in some marriage of convenience and routine.

Where are you now, overweight and just as ugly as your heart was to me.

Where are you now, in a job you're too afraid to leave.

My creative flow has given me a voice, you made me who I am today.

I was once a soft gentle soul, too afraid to live my life.

To all those people that told me I was going nowhere.

To all those people that decided my failure was all of my making.

To those who never looked at me, all because I didn't follow any crowd.

I could hate you for taking me to places where I felt no love.

I could destroy your life as you once did to me.

This is not my way, your life is grey and empty.

Your life was given the karma you deserve, unhappiness in yourself.

Creative artists everywhere all have suffered for their art sometimes.

Creative hearts let's all stay strong, when we are together we all just belong in our unique path of colours,

Everyone out there with such unique flair, let off your fireworks in the air.

All those hurtful people, you're the ones I feel pity for.

My creative art now creates such depth to its expression.

All because once upon a time people broke into my heart and shattered it into a million pieces.

Now all those pieces you once destroyed I've made into a collection of art and beauty.

My creative heart is here to stay, my unique expression grows by the day.

All creative hearts suffer hate, hate turned inside out forms beauty in its place.

Creative love found everywhere has a story to tell.

Creative love is here for my creation from my imagination.

All of my heart's intentions are expressed by my very
own unique art in the forms of words of poetry.
Creative hearts suffer for their art, suffer for talent to
grow.

Burning This Candle Flame Just For Someone

You left in the middle of the night, without warning
you were taken from this life.

Everyone loses someone, sometimes leaving the ones
in the land of the living to pick up the pieces.

Death of anyone you have ever lost, you will know
what it's like when the every part of you becomes
numb.

Reality has a sense of cruelty in being the one left
behind, I would trade my life for a moment with
you.

Anyone out there who knows the pain of losing
someone will know it always feels unjustified.

Leaves the living with a heart shattered and a mind in
pieces to repair.

Take time in this journey that no one is ever ready to
face.

Burning this candle flame just for someone you lost one
time.

Burning this candle flame sends a scent of feelings of
hurt we hold into the places unknown to us.

Energy is what we are made of, I don't believe in the
death of a soul just a body out of its operation and
transferred to live in some other form, some other
place.

Burn a candle, reflect and remember you had loved the
person you lost to the cruelty of death to resend
someplace new.

I feel a sense of you watching over me in a place that
can't harm you, I hope you feel peace there.

The rain I feel inside this heart kills me, knowing we
have finished this journey for now.

You left without knowing how much I loved you.

You left with no warning to save these tears from
falling.

Burning this candle flame for all the passing on people who leave us.

Burning this candle flame for everyone who ever ended the journey to start a new adventure without us in it.

Sometimes I sense you in the places I now go, I hope you see me and smile so.

Sometimes I sense you at night, it makes me feel warm to know you could be close but unseen.

Sometimes I wish I was in the passing with you, but I must finish my journey too just as you did.

Burn a candle full of flames and full of love for anyone who has left your heart without warning.

This flame you left inside my heart, this life I continue to live.

I live it well by the influence you had upon me and the times you showed me what it is to live.

Now I carry on living and carry on loving, till I will one day join you in the unknown place you now reside in, between the life we once shared and the place you travelled to the day you left without warning.

This candle inside my heart will burn forever from the day we were torn apart from the same reality together.

www.ingramcontent.com/pod-product-compliance
Lightning Source LLC
Chambersburg PA
CBHW021156090426
42740CB00008B/1116